WJEC Level 1/2 Vocational Award
HOSPITALITY & CATERING

Bev Saunder
Yvonne Mackey

EXAM PRACTICE WORKBOOK

The Publishers would like to thank the following for permission to reproduce copyright material.

Photo credits

p. 27 l t-b © Parilov/stock.adobe.com, © Aleksei Lazukov/stock.adobe.com, © Izikmd/stock.adobe.com, © John Vlahidis/Wirestock/stock.adobe.com, **p.39** © Ammit/stock.adobe.com, **p.41** © Olga/stock.adobe.com, **p.47** © Jusep/stock.adobe.com

Although every effort has been made to ensure that website addresses are correct at time of going to press, Hodder Education cannot be held responsible for the content of any website mentioned in this book. It is sometimes possible to find a relocated web page by typing in the address of the home page for a website in the URL window of your browser.

Hachette UK's policy is to use papers that are natural, renewable and recyclable products and made from wood grown in well-managed forests and other controlled sources. The logging and manufacturing processes are expected to conform to the environmental regulations of the country of origin.

To order, please visit www.hoddereducation.com or contact Customer Service at education@hachette.co.uk / +44 (0)1235 827827.

ISBN: 978 1 0360 0669 3

© Bev Saunder, Yvonne Mackey 2024

First published in 2024 by Hodder Education (a trading division of Hodder & Stoughton Limited),
An Hachette UK Company
Carmelite House
50 Victoria Embankment
London EC4Y 0DZ

www.hoddereducation.com

The authorised representative in the EEA is Hachette Ireland, 8 Castlecourt Centre, Dublin 15, D15 XTP3, Ireland (email: info@hbgi.ie)

Impression number 10 9 8 7 6 5 4 3 2

Year 2028 2027 2026 2025

All rights reserved. Apart from any use permitted under UK copyright law, no part of this publication may be reproduced or transmitted in any form or by any means, electronic or mechanical, including photocopying and recording, or held within any information storage and retrieval system, without permission in writing from the publisher or under licence from the Copyright Licensing Agency Limited. Further details of such licences (for reprographic reproduction) may be obtained from the Copyright Licensing Agency Limited, www.cla.co.uk

Illustrations by Aptara Inc.

Typeset in India by Aptara Inc.

Printed by Ashford Colour ltd, UK

A catalogue record for this title is available from the British Library.

Contents

1.1 Hospitality and catering provision — 5
   Recall activities — 5
   Short-answer exam-style practice questions — 10
   Long-answer exam-style practice questions — 14

1.2 How hospitality and catering provisions operate — 22
   Recall activities — 22
   Short-answer exam-style practice questions — 26
   Long-answer exam-style practice questions — 30

1.3 Health and safety in hospitality and catering — 38
   Recall activities — 38
   Short-answer exam-style practice questions — 45
   Long-answer exam-style practice questions — 50

1.4 Food safety in hospitality and catering — 55
   Recall activities — 55
   Short-answer exam-style practice questions — 60
   Long-answer exam-style practice questions — 64

WJEC Level 1/2 Vocational Award Hospitality and Catering Exam Practice Workbook

Introduction

This workbook will help you prepare to tackle exam questions for your WJEC Level 1/2 Vocational Award in Hospitality and Catering (Technical Award) Unit 1 exam.

The exam lasts for 1 hour and 20 minutes and is worth 80 marks.

You will be tested on the following topic areas:
- 1.1 Hospitality and catering provision.
- 1.2 How hospitality and catering provisions operate
- 1.3 Health and safety in hospitality and catering
- 1.4 Food safety in hospitality and catering.

Questions may focus on one topic area or might require answers that combine information from two or more topic areas.

Features to help you succeed

Each topic area starts with **recall activities** that will help you to remember important information you will need when answering exam questions. These activities include crosswords, quizzes, matching exercises and filling in missing words in tables, sentences or diagrams.

Some short-answer and long-answer questions include **hints and tips** next to them to give you extra advice on how to approach them. They may suggest key points to consider when answering the question, explain what important words included in the question mean, or give guidance on common mistakes candidates make when answering these types of questions.

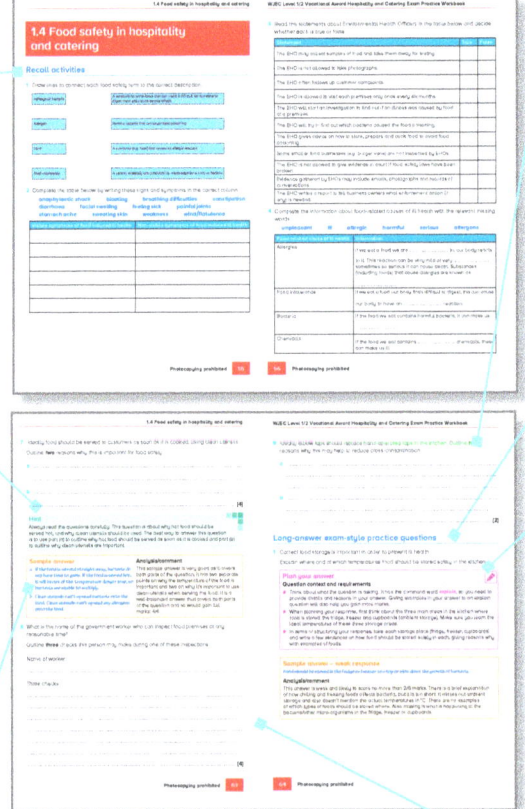

Short-answer exam practice questions help you to practice answering multiple-choice and short-answer exam questions that are typically worth 1–6 marks.

Longer-answer exam practice questions will help you to practice answering extended response questions typically worth 6–8 marks. These questions will sometimes include a context or scenario.

Some questions will also include a series of stages or activities to support you as you answer the question. They may identify and explain key words for you, have headings, bullet points or mind maps for you to complete to help you to plan and structure your answer or include partially completed answers.

Example student answers or extracts from student answers are provided for some questions. These will help you understand how to gain the most marks and may ask you to think about the strengths and weaknesses of the answer and how it could be improved.

All questions will have **spaces for you to write or plan your answers.**

Answers to all questions are available online at www.hoddereducation.com/wjec-vocational-award-hospitality-workbook-answers

1.1 Hospitality and catering provision

Recall activities

1 Draw lines to match each member of the kitchen brigade with their role.

Kitchen assistant	Has responsibility for a particular section of the menu or an area of the kitchen
Pastry chef	Also called head chef; in charge of the kitchen
Executive chef	Makes breads, pastries, cakes, batters and desserts
Chef de partie	Supports the chef by washing up, sorting and preparing ingredients

2 Fill in the crossword with words related to different types of food service using the clues provided.

ACROSS
3 A waiter uses a spoon and a fork to serve food (6, 7)
5 Sit-down meal for a formal event (7)
6 Food cooked quickly to eat in or take away (4, 4)

DOWN
1 Place where customer chooses their food, pays for it, then sits down to eat it (9)
2 Food served from a side table or trolley, usually for dramatic effect (8)
4 A selection of dishes where customers can help themselves (6)

3 Different types of costs have an impact on the success of a hospitality and catering business.

Complete the sentences below using the words provided.

consumables   fixed   labour   material
overheads   rent   variables

.... costs are the salaries and wages for all staff connected to the business.

.... costs are the cost of things like food and drink, ... such as napkins, and cleaning materials.

.... are costs that are connected to materials or labour, for example

................................, energy, water, telephone, internet, Wi-Fi, insurance, furniture and furnishings.

Costs can also be split into:

.... costs – costs that can change depending on the amount of business the establishment does, such as the cost of food and drink.

.... costs – costs that are always the same, such as rent, insurance and energy.

4 Which **one** of these is an example of a commercial residential establishment?

   a café
   b coffee shop
   c public house
   d Airbnb

1.1 Hospitality and catering provision

5 Complete the mind map with the **five** types of employment contract.

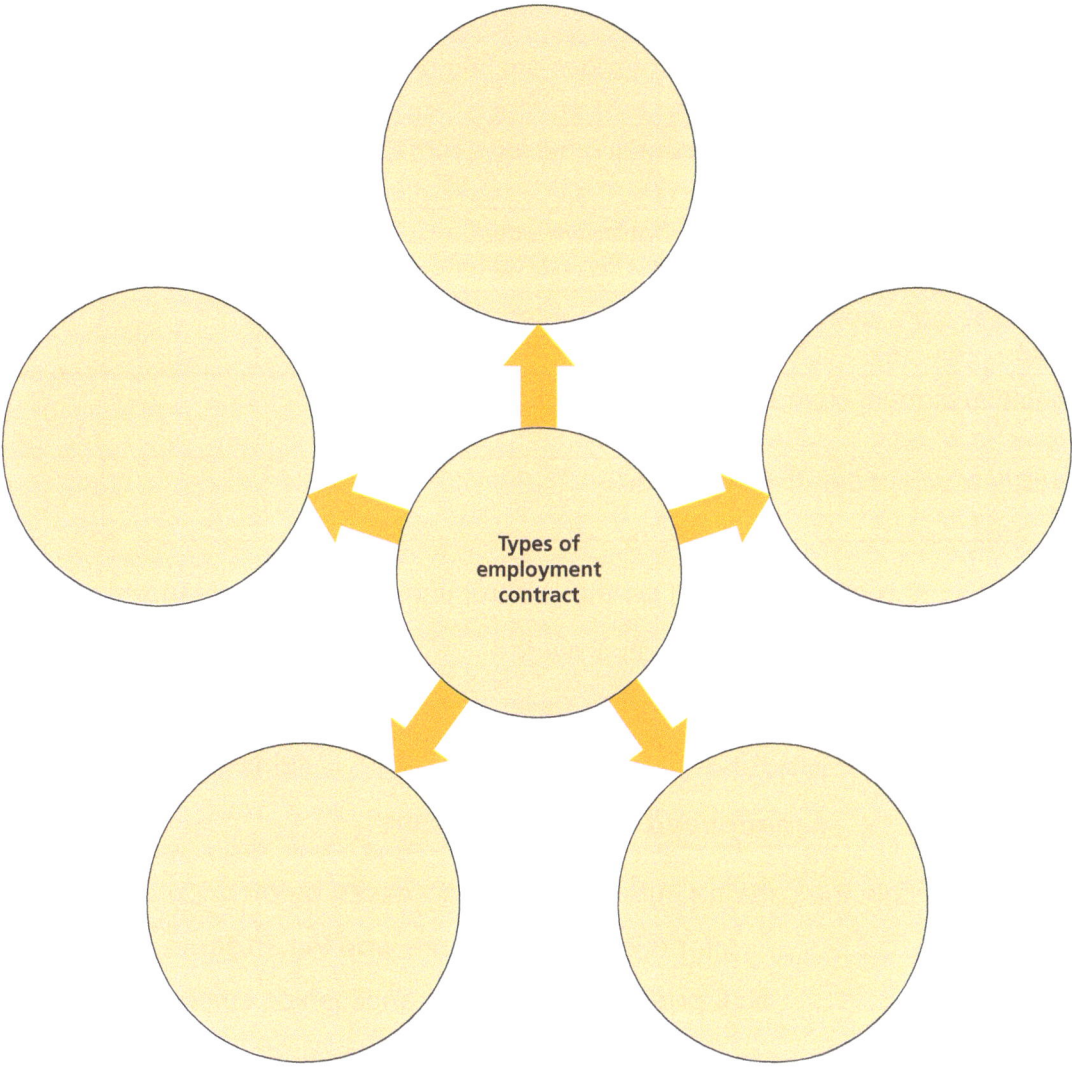

6 Draw lines to match the key term with the correct definition.

Key term	Definition
Hospitality	Camping that offers more luxurious facilities than traditional camping
Catering	Food ordered and delivered to your room in an establishment such as a hotel
Beverage	Providing accommodation, food and drinks in a variety of places outside of the home
Glamping	The team of people who work in the kitchen with each one having a clear role
Room service	A drink other than water
Front of house	The part of hospitality and catering businesses where employees have direct face-to-face contact with customers
Kitchen brigade	Providing food and drink services to a customer

7 Complete the table below by ticking whether each statement is true or false.

Statement	True	False
An example of a commercial residential provider is a bed and breakfast.		
An example of a commercial non-residential provider is Airbnb.		
A suite in a hotel has a bedroom and a bathroom only.		
A Michelin three stars means the standard of cuisine will be exceptional.		
A chambermaid or room attendant prepares rooms for guests.		
A head waiter is part of the kitchen brigade.		

8 Apprenticeships are a combination of on-the-job training and classroom learning.

Complete the sentences using the words provided

apprenticeship   **college**   **five**   **mentor**

train   **practical**   **wages**   **skills**

study   **experienced**   **qualification**

Many of the jobs within the catering industry can be accessed by an .... This means you .... for a job while you are working. In some cases, you may also attend .... on a part-time basis. Apprenticeships combine .... training in a job with .... They take between one and .... years to complete.

As an apprentice, you will:

○ earn ...., including holiday pay

○ work with .... staff

○ have a .... to support you

○ learn new .... needed for the job

○ study for a related .... (could be day-release).

1.1 Hospitality and catering provision

9 Complete the table below with the definitions of different types of counter service. One has been done for you.

Type of counter service	Description
Cafeteria	
Buffet	A selection of dishes is laid out on a table or counter for a customer to help themselves. There are different styles of buffets.
Sit-down buffet	
Stand-up or fork buffet	
Finger buffet	
Fast food	

WJEC Level 1/2 Vocational Award Hospitality and Catering Exam Practice Workbook

Short-answer exam-style practice questions

1 Poppy is a server working at a café.
   She has a zero-hours contract.

   a State **one** advantage of a zero-hours contract.

   .... [1]

   b State **one** disadvantage of a zero-hours contract.

   .... [1]

2 The Hills Hotel needs to hire a head housekeeper.

   Name and describe **two** personal attributes that a head housekeeper should have.

   a Personal attribute 1:

   ....

   ....

   ....

   b Personal attribute 2:

   ....

   ....

   .... [4]

> **Hint**
> Be careful when answering a question that says **state**. State means give only the main facts, but those facts should be expressed clearly and fully. It does not require a long explanation. A good indicator is how many lines are available for your answer.

Sample answer

Personal attribute 1: good communicator

A head housekeeper should be able to communicate well with other people.

Personal attribute 2: hygienic

A head housekeeper should have high standards of hygiene as they represent the hotel. For example, their hair should be clean and well styled, and their uniform should be smart and clean.

Analysis/comment

Correctly identifying a relevant personal attribute and giving a very brief description of what it means will score one mark. For the full two marks, the description should contain more detail. This answer would achieve 3/4.

To improve this answer, for the first attribute (a good communicator), the student could have included an example of what good communication would look like, such as reference to a relevant type of communication: verbal/listening skills/non-verbal/written.

The second attribute (hygienic) would be awarded the full two marks for correctly identifying the attribute and a full description of what hygienic means in this context.

1.1 Hospitality and catering provision

3 Explain what is meant by the term 'commercial residential establishments'.

....

....

....

.... [2]

4 List **four** facilities a hotel may offer its customers.

a ....

b ....

c ....

d .... [4]

5 State **two** ways in which a hotel can reduce its energy and water consumption.

a ....

....

b ....

.... [2]

6 Identify **two** different types of media a restaurant could use to attract new customers.

....

....

....

.... [2]

7 Describe the impact on a business of a weak economy.

....

....

....

.... [2]

8 Name **four** different types of rooms you could choose from when booking an overnight stay.

a ....

b ....

c ....

d .... **[4]**

9 State **two** reasons why it is important to follow an efficient workflow pattern in a catering kitchen.

a ....

....

b ....

.... **[2]**

10 The Hills Hotel needs to hire a head chef. Name and describe **two** personal attributes that a head chef should have.

a Personal attribute 1:

....

....

....

....

b Personal attribute 2:

....

....

....

.... **[4]**

1.1 Hospitality and catering provision

11 Explain what a customer would expect from a restaurant that has one AA rosette award.

Hint
Remember to read the question carefully – in this instance it asks you to **explain** what is meant by **one** rosette award (remember there are five and each one is different).

....

....

....

.... [2]

12 State **three** items that could be included in a full English breakfast.

a ....

b ....

c .... [3]

13 List **three** leisure facilities you may find in a high-end hotel.

a ....

b ....

c .... [3]

14 State **three** benefits of a vending machine as a method of food service.

a ....

   ....

b ....

   ....

c ....

   .... [3]

Photocopying prohibited

Long-answer exam-style practice questions

1 Nisha has set up a mobile van selling a variety of hot and cold beverages at a car park near a nature reserve. She is aware of the need to be environmentally friendly.

Explain how Nisha can ensure that her business is environmentally friendly.

Plan your answer

Question context and requirements

- Think about what the question is asking. The question has the command word **explain**, so you need to set out the facts and the reasons for them, include some detail and make them plain and clear.
- When planning your response, first think about the scenario. It's a mobile van serving a variety of beverages — what does the word beverage mean? (It means a drink other than water.) The measures to make sure the business is environmentally friendly need to be relevant to a mobile van selling hot and cold drinks.
- When you are structuring your response, consider which environmental measures would be the most relevant. Make a quick note of them then explain each measure in a separate paragraph, relating it to the scenario.

Sample answer

Nisha can make sure she provides a bin so that any litter can be disposed of in the right way.

She could use recyclable materials for her cups and cutlery.

She could use technology to take orders so she does not have to use paper.

Analysis/comment

This answer is likely to score 3/6 marks. The explanation is good, showing some knowledge and understanding. However, it is almost a list and although three correct measures have been identified, they have not been fully explained.

As an example of how this answer could be improved, the second point could be expanded on to mention using paper straws, bamboo cutlery, and cardboard recyclable cups and lids.

Now write your own answer.

[6]

2 There are many ways in which food can be served, including at a table, at a counter, or directly to a person (personal service).

Describe **four** types of personal service.

> **Plan your answer**
>
> **Question context and requirements**
> - Think about what the question is asking. The question has the command word **describe**, so you need to write about all the main features.
> - When planning your response, first think about the scenario. The question is about how food is served; specifically, how food is served directly to a customer.
> - When you are structuring your response, consider the four types of personal service. Make a quick note of them, then describe each type in a separate paragraph.
> - The four types of personal service are:
>   – home delivery
>   – takeaway restaurants
>   – tray or trolley
>   – vending machines.
> - Now take each type of personal service and describe how a customer would obtain their food.

Now write your own answer.

....
....
....
....
....
....
....
....
....
....
....
....
....
.... [8]

3 Describe the ways in which digital technology is used in the hospitality and catering industry.

[8]

4 Explain the importance of monitoring the competition when running a restaurant business.

[8]

5 Describe **four** different types of table service.

....

[8]

6 Describe the role of an executive chef.

[6]

7 Discuss how each of the following employment contracts works:

- casual
- seasonal
- zero-hours
- full-time.

[8]

1.2 How hospitality and catering provisions operate

Recall activities

1 Draw lines to match each utensil with what it is used for.

Wok		Lifting food off a baking sheet
Balloon whisk		Stir-frying food
Palette knife		Whisking; adding air to a mixture
Rolling pin		Glazing
Pastry brush		Rolling out a pastry or a dough

2 The table below describes how different acts of legislation protect people. Insert the correct words from the list to complete the sentences.

as described   GDPR   2015   consent   information   equality
disability   data   religion   compensation   protection

Act of legislation	How this legislation protects people
The Consumer .... Act 1987	This gives you the right to claim .... from the producer of a defective product if it has caused damage, death or personal injury.
The Consumer Rights Act	This act states that all products must be: • of satisfactory quality • fit for purpose • ....
The UK General Data Protection Regulation	States that when you buy goods and services, stay at a hotel or sometimes even just visit a website, the organisations you deal with may collect .... and .... about you, such as your name, address and date of birth. Under .... rules, businesses must have a customer's .... to store this information, use it for marketing purposes or share it with other businesses.
The .... Act 2010	This act protects customers from direct discrimination on the basis of: • age • .... • gender reassignment • pregnancy, maternity and breastfeeding • race – this includes ethnic or national origins, colour and nationality • .... or belief • marriage or civil partnership • sex and sexual orientation.

1.2 How hospitality and catering provisions operate

3 Hospitality and catering provisions have to adapt to meet the needs of an ever-changing customer climate.

Complete the mind map with the **four** main customer requirements and needs.

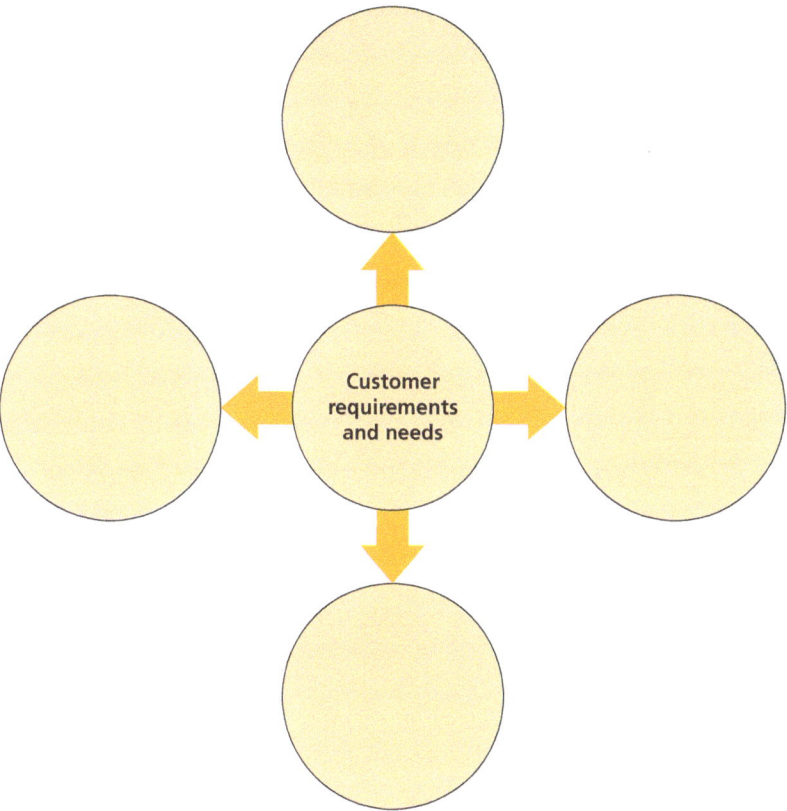

4 The terms listed below show the stages of an efficient workflow for a catering kitchen.

Put the **six** terms below into the correct order. Write a number from 1–6 next to each term, starting with 1 for the first stage.

Food preparation	☐
Dishing up and service	☐
Receipt of goods	☐
Storing goods	☐
Checking and weighing goods	☐
Cooking	☐

Photocopying prohibited   23

5 Fill in the crossword with words related to different types of equipment using the clues provided.

ACROSS
2 Used for mixing and folding (7)
6 Used for stir-frying food (3)
7 Used for cooking food in an oven (6, 5)
8 Used for glazing (6, 5)
9 Used for removing lumps from icing sugar or flour (5)

DOWN
1 Used for adding air to a mixture (7, 5)
3 Used for lifting food off a baking sheet (7, 5)
4 Used for draining liquid (8)
5 Used for mashing and eating (4)
8 Used for removing the skin from fruit and vegetables (6)

6 Complete this mind map identifying the **five** areas which the front of house covers.

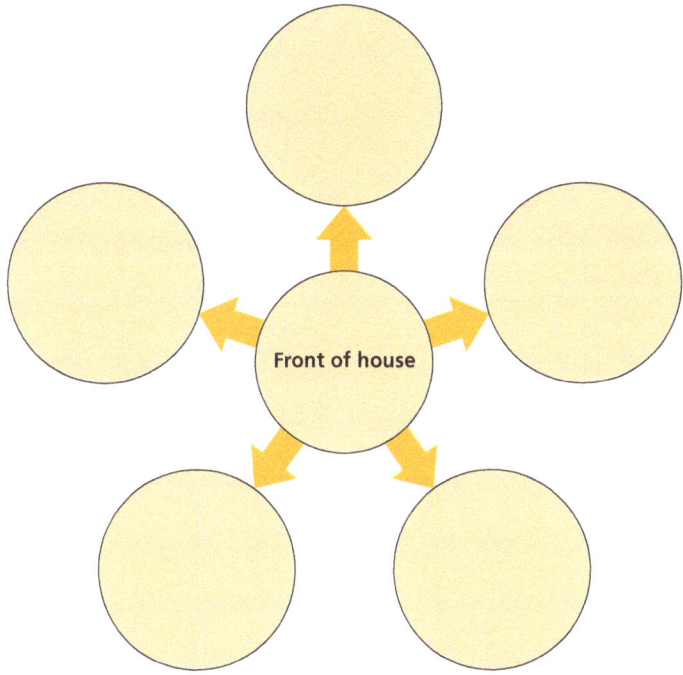

7 List **seven** materials for cleaning that are used frequently in a catering kitchen.

a ....

b ....

c ....

d ....

e ....

f ....

g ....

8 Draw lines to match the key term with the correct definition.

Key term	Definition
Workflow	The practice of using the product with the shortest shelf life before using a similar one with a longer shelf life
Stock rotation	First in, first out policy used to ensure older stock gets used up first
Stock	Bill sent to someone for goods or services they have received
FIFO	A set of rules specifying the type of clothing to be worn
Invoice	All materials, ingredients and equipment used
Dress code	The requirements of a specific or restricted diet
Dietary needs	The flow of food and drinks from the kitchen to the customer

9 These terms show the stages of an efficient workflow for the front of house.

Put the **seven** terms into the correct order. Write a number from 1–7 by each term, starting with 1 for the first stage.

Take drinks and food order	☐
Serve meal	☐
Meet and greet customer, show them to their table	☐
Serve desserts/coffee	☐
Clear table, issue bill	☐
Reset table for next customer	☐
Clear table, offer desserts, coffee	☐

Short-answer exam-style practice questions

1 Explain how a wet bain-marie keeps food warm.

....

....

....

.... [2]

2 Define the term 'toque'.

....

.... [1]

3 Name **two** items you would expect to see in a first-aid kit in a catering kitchen.

a ....

b .... [2]

4 State **two** catering considerations a tourist might have when booking a place to stay.

a ....

b .... [2]

1.2 How hospitality and catering provisions operate

5 State **four** safety materials that are used in a catering kitchen.

a ....

b ....

c ....

d .... [4]

6 Fill in the table below by ticking whether each statement is true or false.

Statement	True	False
The front of house covers reception and counter service.		
Good kitchen workflow helps with efficiency.		
FIFO is a system to ensure new stock is used first.		
All materials, ingredients and equipment used in a catering kitchen are referred to as stock.		

[4]

7 Identify the following pieces of equipment.

Image	Name of equipment
	a ....
	b ....
	c ....
	d ....

[4]

8 Outline **four** ways in which a hotel can ensure it is accessible to all customers.

a ....

....

b ....

....

c ....

....

d ....

....[4]

9 Describe the uniform that you would expect a member of the front-of-house staff to wear.

....

....

....

....

....

....

....

....

....

....[4]

Hint

As this is a **describe** question, it is important not to just list what a front-of-house staff member should wear. As there are four marks for the question, it should be a detailed description. Note too that the question refers to a front-of-house staff member, not a member of the catering kitchen staff.

Sample answer

Staff should wear a uniform that will help customers identify them. It should have a logo of the company, and the staff member should have a name badge too. They should be smart and clean as they are representing the company and it needs to have a positive image. The uniform should be comfortable for the member of staff to work in as they will often work long hours.

Analysis/comment

This answer would be awarded 4/4 as it successfully describes a number of points. Each point has been accurately described — for example, the uniform should have a logo and name badge to help the customer identify the staff member.

10 Explain the use of the following pieces of equipment.

Piece of equipment	What it is used for
Floor-standing mixer	
Steamer	
Hot plate/pass	
Glass chiller	

[8]

11 Customer requirements continue to change and evolve. Hospitality and catering establishments need to keep up with current trends in order to be competitive.

Identify and explain **four** current trends.

Hint

You will receive **one** mark for identifying each trend and **one** mark for each explanation.

a Trend

....

o Explanation

....

....

b Trend

....

o Explanation

....

....

WJEC Level 1/2 Vocational Award Hospitality and Catering Exam Practice Workbook

c Trend

....

o Explanation

....

....

d Trend

....

o Explanation

....

....[8]

Long-answer exam-style practice questions

1 Explain how a hotel in Bristol could meet the needs of a business person who is staying there for a few days to attend meetings.

Plan your answer

Question context and requirements

- Think about what the question is asking. The question has the command word **explain**, so you need to set out the facts and the reasons for them, including some detail, and make these plain and clear.
- When planning your response, look carefully at the scenario. An explanation is needed as to what are the needs of a person who is on business and staying in a hotel — what might they need from a hotel?
- When you are structuring your response, consider what the needs of a business person are. Make a quick note of them then explain each need in a separate paragraph and say how the hotel can meet that need.

Sample answer

A hotel would need to provide the following to meet the needs of a business person.

Free Wi-Fi so they can work on their computer at the hotel and make calls. They might want to do Zoom meetings too.

It would be useful to have a desk and chair to work from in their room, with plug sockets and charging points.

They may need to use a conference or meeting room so it would be useful if one were available to them.

Analysis/comment

This answer would score 3/6 marks. The explanation included has a good level of detail, but there are not sufficient points for six marks. The student has focused on the business person's work needs but not looked at their wider needs, for instance their potential need for food and beverages, or access to laundry facilities and leisure facilities, such as a gym or swimming pool, if they are working all day.

1.2 How hospitality and catering provisions operate

Now write your own answer.

....

[6]

2 Different types of customers may have different requirements for accommodation.

Describe **four** types of customers and their needs when booking accommodation.

> **Plan your answer**
>
> **Question context and requirements**
> - Think about what the question is asking. The question has the command word **describe**, so you need write about all of the main features.
> - When planning your response, first think about the scenario. The question is about what the customer needs for accommodation are.
> - When you are structuring your response, consider which are the four types of customer. Make a quick note of them:
>   – budget travellers
>   – business people
>   – families
>   – tourist travelling for leisure.
> - Now take each type of customer and describe what their accommodation needs are. Remember, every type of customer has different accommodation needs, so try not to repeat answers.

Now write your own answer.

....

....

....

....

....

....

....

....

....

....

....

....

....

....

....

[8]

3 Describe the acts of legislation that aim to protect customers in the hospitality and catering industry.

[8]

4 Describe how you would make sure your restaurant is accessible and safe for people who use a wheelchair.

....

[6]

5 A chef should look clean and professional. Explain the dress code requirements for a chef.

[8]

6 Meeting customers' needs is very important to the success of a business. Describe the customer needs a catering establishment would need to consider.

.... [6]

7 Choose **four** pieces of large kitchen equipment that could be used in a catering kitchen. Describe what each piece of equipment is used for.

....
....
....
....
....
....
....
....
....
....
....
....
....
....
....
....
....
....
....
....
....
....
....
.... **[8]**

1.3 Health and safety in hospitality and catering

Recall activities

1 Complete the table below with the names of the acts being described and a summary of the act. The first one has been done for you.

Act of legislation	How this legislation protects people	Summary of act
Control of Substances Hazardous to Health Regulations 2002 (COSHH)	Covers substances that are hazardous to health, for example chemicals, fumes, vapours and gases. An employer should ensure that employee use of and exposure to these substances is kept to a minimum, and that they are trained to use these substances.	This act includes substances hazardous to health. Exposure to these substances should be kept to a minimum and training given to employees.
	Employers are responsible for providing a .... workplace that will not cause illness or harm to their .... Employees must ensure that they: • work in a safe way and don't put themselves or others in .... • report anything that is a health and safety ...., or something that could be a risk.	
	These regulations protect employees from injury or .... when they are lifting or moving heavy equipment or awkwardly .... items.	

38 Photocopying prohibited

1.3 Health and safety in hospitality and catering

Act of legislation	How this legislation protects people	Summary of act
	Personal protective equipment (PPE) is ………………… or equipment designed to protect the wearer from …………………………….. These regulations require employers to provide suitable …………………………… protective clothing and equipment to employees who may be exposed to a …………………………… to their health and safety while at work.	
	As part of the Health and ………………………… at Work etc. Act 1974 (see above), these ………………………… require employers to report certain workplace ………………………… to the Health and Safety Executive (HSE).	

2 The image below shows a butcher cutting meat.

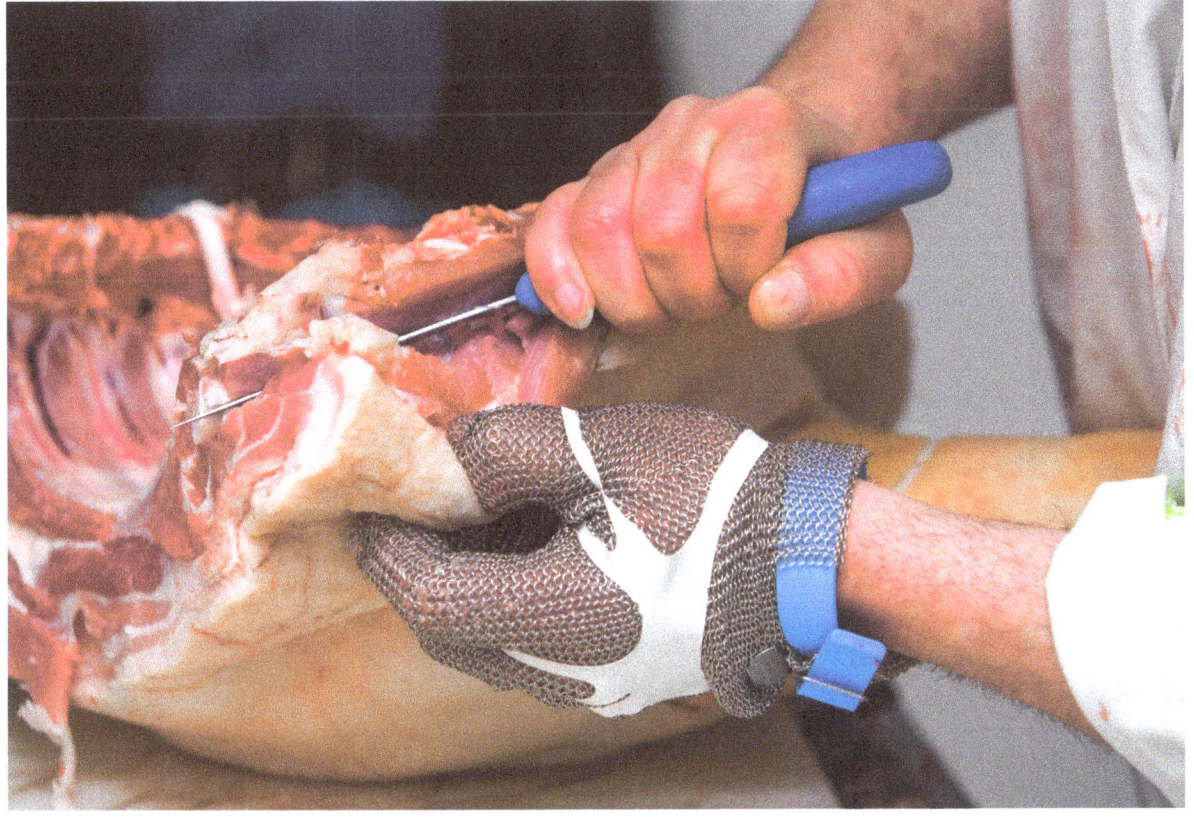

How do the following laws protect employees who cut meat as part of their job?

a Health and Safety at Work etc. Act 1974:

....

....

....

....

....

....

....

....

b Personal Protective Equipment at Work Regulations (PPER) 1992:

....

....

....

....

....

....

....

....

3 Draw lines to match each term to the correct description.

Term	Description
Hazard	How likely it is that someone could be harmed by a hazard
Control	Something that could cause harm
Risk	A way of reducing the risk of a hazard causing harm

4 When handling boxes, cartons and trays, there is a correct way to lift.

Using the accompanying images to help you, fill in the table below by ticking whether each statement is true or false.

Statement	True	False
Always keep your back straight.		
Keep your knees straight and use the strength from your back.		
Always reach forwards.		
Keep the item as far away from your body as possible.		
Use protective clothing if there are sharp edges on boxes or cartons.		
Never attempt to carry items that are too heavy – always get help.		

5 Use the clues to fill in the crossword.

ACROSS

6 The UK agency responsible for health and safety (6, 3, 6, 9)
7 A way of reducing the risk of a hazard causing harm (7)

DOWN

1 What does PPE stand for? (8, 10, 9)
2 A butcher could wear............................ gloves when using sharp knives to cut meat (10)
3 A way of identifying things that could cause harm in the workplace (4, 10)
4 Risky or dangerous (9)
5 How likely it is that someone could be harmed by a hazard (4)

1.3 Health and safety in hospitality and catering

6 Fill in the gaps using the words provided.

dangerous   **safety**   **government**   **identifying**   **public**   **enforcement**
written   **equipment**   **welfare**   **employer**   **injury**

Hazardous means something that is risky or ....

A risk assessment is a way of .... things that could cause harm to people in the workplace.

A health and safety policy statement is a .... statement by an

.... of its commitment to health and .... for its employees and

the ....

Personal protective equipment (PPE) is clothing or .... designed to protect the

wearer from ....

The Health and Safety Executive (HSE) is a UK .... agency responsible for

the .... and regulation of workplace, health, safety and ....

7 Complete the table by placing these steps to a risk assessment into the correct order in the table below:

Identify the hazard

Statements
- Review the assessment and update if necessary
- Decide who might be harmed and how
- Record the findings and implement them
- Evaluate the risks and decide on the controls needed

Step	Place the statements in the correct order
1	
2	
3	
4	

Photocopying prohibited

8 The text below explains how to calculate risks when writing a risk assessment. Fill in the gaps using the words provided:

multiplied   **calculate**   **low**   **risk**   **hazard**   **possible**   **scale**

It is possible to ………………… whether a level of risk is high, medium or

…………………. To do this, the severity of the ………………… and the likelihood of it

happening are given a score on a ………………… of 1–5. These figures can then be

………………… together to give a level of …………………. The overall aim is to remove

or reduce the risk to an acceptable level, as close to 1 as ………………….

9 Complete the table on the levels of risk.

………………… risk 8	………………… risk 8–14	………………… risk 15–25
Continue to ………………… regularly to ensure ………………… remain …………………..	Continue but implement extra ………………… where possible and monitor ……………………..	………………… the activity! Identify new controls Activity must not ………………… until risks are ………………… to a low or ………………… level

10 Fill in the table on accident forms by ticking whether each statement is true or false.

Statement	True	False
If the HSE is investigating an accident, it will want to see a record of it.		
It is optional for a business to have an accident book.		
An accident record form should include the date, time and location.		
An accident record form must include the treatment given.		
It is not necessary to explain how to prevent such an accident happening again.		

1.3 Health and safety in hospitality and catering

Short-answer exam-style practice questions

1 State what is meant by a risk assessment.

   ....

   .... [1]

2 Identify **one** physical hazard and **one** chemical hazard that would need to be included in a food safety management plan.

   a Physical hazard:

      ....

   b Chemical hazard:

      .... [2]

3 Identify **two** conditions that bacteria need to grow.

   a ....

   b .... [2]

4 State **two** pieces of information that should be recorded in a record system for the running of a restaurant kitchen.

   a ....

   b .... [2]

5 List the **five** steps to a risk assessment.

   a ....

   b ....

   c ....

   d ....

   e .... [5]

Hint

Be careful when answering a question that says *list*. 'List' means short pieces of information, so you should only write the facts; the answer does not require a long explanation. A good indicator is how many lines are available for your answer. In this case there are five lines and the question is worth five marks – one mark for each point listed.

6 State **two** pieces of information that need to be included on an accident form.

   a ....

   ....

   b ....

   .... [2]

7 Identify **two** substances that could be considered hazards to health.

   a ....

   b .... [2]

8 Explain what is meant by a health and safety statement.

   ....

   ....

   ....

   .... [2]

9 Explain what is meant by a food safety management system.

   ....

   ....

   ....

   ....

   ....

   ....

   ....

   ....

   .... [4]

1.3 Health and safety in hospitality and catering

10 Give **two** examples of PPE and explain how each would protect the employee.

....

....

....

....

....

....

....

....

.... [4]

Sample answer
PPE is personal protective equipment, for example wearing gloves.

Analysis/comment

This answer would be awarded 1/4. The question does not ask what PPE is, it asks for examples of it. The example given is correct but there is no explanation of how the gloves would protect the employee.

To improve this answer, it should have included an explanation of how wearing gloves protects an employee, and the question asked for two examples not just one.

Hint
It is so important to read the question carefully before answering it. In question 10, it is important to note that examples of PPE are needed, not a definition of PPE. Check how many examples are needed. In this instance it is two examples; the number is usually highlighted in bold.

11 Complete the table by matching the COSHH symbol with its meaning

acute toxicity   health hazard   corrosive   explosive
hazardous to the environment   flammable

Symbol	Meaning
!	
corrosive symbol	
skull and crossbones	
flame	
exploding bomb	
environment	

[6]

12 State **four** reasons why it is important that the employees are offered health and safety training.

a ....

....

b ....

....

c ....

....

d ....

.... **[4]**

13 Zara is a waitress in a large hotel. She has slipped on a water spillage in the dining room and has sprained her ankle. Complete the accident form below.

Details of the accident	
What caused the accident?	
How could the accident have been prevented?	
What further action should be taken?	

[6]

14 State **two** potential risks to the health and security of:

Hint
Do not repeat your answers as this will not gain marks.

a Employees ....

....

.... **[2]**

b Suppliers ....

....

.... **[2]**

c Customers ....

....

.... **[2]**

1.3 Health and safety in hospitality and catering

15 Describe **two** opening checks the owner of a catering business would carry out as part of the Safer food, better business (SFBB) food safety management plan.

> **Hint**
> Read questions 15 and 16 carefully to note the subtle difference – question 15 is asking about opening checks, question 16 is asking about closing checks.

a ....

....

....

b ....

....

....

.... [4]

16 Describe **two** closing checks the owner of a catering business would carry out as part of the Safer food, better business (SFBB) food safety management plan.

a ....

....

....

b ....

....

....

.... [4]

17 Explain the term 'critical limit'.

....

....

....

.... [2]

18 Explain the term 'due diligence'.

....

....

....

.... [2]

Long-answer exam-style practice questions

1 Describe the safety responsibilities of an employer under the Health and Safety at Work etc. Act 1974

Plan your answer

Question context and requirements

- Think about what the question is asking. It has the command word **describe**, which means you will need to write out the main features of the safety responsibilities of an employer under the Health and Safety at Work etc. Act 1974.
- When planning your response, check whether it is asking you to focus on the employer or employee – in this case, it's the employer. Check which act of legislation it is referring to – in this case, it is the Health and Safety at Work etc. Act 1974. Make notes of the key features of this act, referring to the employer only.
- The act has six points that an employer has to ensure they follow – this is a good way to structure your response. Describe each point in turn.

Sample answer

The employer has to make sure they do risk assessments to make sure everything is safe. They need to train staff so they don't have accidents. They need to check electrical equipment.

Analysis/comment

This answer is likely to achieve 2/6. This student hasn't included all six points, and the descriptions of the points they have included aren't detailed enough – they only show a basic knowledge.

To improve this answer, the student could write about each point in more detail and give an example. For instance: 'An employer needs to ensure that all staff have health and safety training so that they can use equipment and handle food safely. This training should be updated regularly.'

Now write your own answer.

....

....

....

....

....

....

.... [6]

1.3 Health and safety in hospitality and catering

2 Potential risks to the health and security of employees, suppliers and customers must be controlled by putting measures in place to ensure that risk is low or medium.

Discuss the potential health and security risks to customers at a restaurant.

....

[8]

3 Describe the control measures that are needed to produce safe food.

[8]

1.3 Health and safety in hospitality and catering

4 Describe the opening and closing checks that would need to be made for a small business using the Safer food, better business (SFBB) management system.

[8]

5 Describe the COSHH Regulations a catering business needs to follow to ensure the safety of its employees.

[6]

1.4 Food safety in hospitality and catering

Recall activities

1 Draw lines to connect each food safety term to the correct description.

Term	Description
Pathogenic bacteria	A sensitivity to some foods that can make it difficult for someone to digest them and can cause side effects
Allergen	Harmful bacteria that can cause food poisoning
Toxin	A substance (e.g. food) that causes an allergic reaction
Food intolerance	A poison, especially one produced by micro-organisms such as bacteria

2 Complete the table below by writing these signs and symptoms in the correct column.

anaphylactic shock   bloating   breathing difficulties   constipation
diarrhoea   facial swelling   feeling sick   painful joints
stomach ache   sweating skin   weakness   wind/flatulence

Visible symptoms of food-induced ill health	Non-visible symptoms of food-induced ill health

3 Read the statements about Environmental Health Officers in the table below and decide whether each is true or false.

Statement	True	False
The EHO may collect samples of food and take them away for testing.		
The EHO is not allowed to take photographs.		
The EHO often follows up customer complaints.		
The EHO is allowed to visit each premises only once every six months.		
The EHO will start an investigation to find out if an illness was caused by food at a premises.		
The EHO will try to find out which bacteria caused the food poisoning.		
The EHO gives advice on how to store, prepare and cook food to avoid food poisoning.		
Some smaller food businesses (e.g. burger vans) are not inspected by EHOs.		
The EHO is not allowed to give evidence in court if food safety laws have been broken.		
Evidence gathered by EHOs may include emails, photographs and records of conversations.		
The EHO writes a report to tell business owners what enforcement action (if any) is needed.		

4 Complete the information about food-related causes of ill health with the relevant missing words.

unpleasant   ill   allergic   harmful   serious   allergens

Food-related cause of ill health	Information
Allergies	If we eat a food we are ……………………… to, our body reacts to it. This reaction can be very mild or very ……………………… sometimes so serious it can cause death. Substances (including foods) that cause allergies are known as ………………………
Food intolerance	If we eat a food our body finds difficult to digest, this can cause our body to have an ……………………… reaction.
Bacteria	If the food we eat contains harmful bacteria, it can make us ……………………… .
Chemicals	If the food we eat contains ……………………… chemicals, these can make us ill.

5 Fill in the table below about food safety and allergies by ticking whether each statement is true or false.

Statement	True	False
Unwashed hands can contaminate food.		
A food allergy is when a person's body reacts in a negative way to a food they have eaten.		
Lupin flour is made from wheat.		
Scallops and oysters are examples of crustaceans.		
Lactose is a sugar found naturally in cereals.		

6 Fill in the crossword with words related to food safety using the clues provided.

ACROSS
5 A piece of equipment used to measure food temperatures (11, 5)
6 Another name for a poison produced by bacteria (5)
7 The name of the expiry date on most perishable foods (3, 2, 4)
8 Ingredients must be listed in descending order by this (6)
9 High-risk foods should be kept out of this temperature range (6, 4)

DOWN
1 Another word for harmful when talking about bacteria (10)
2 Wheat, rye, oats and barley all contain this (6)
3 The most common type of bacterial food poisoning in the UK (13)
4 The allergen group that crabs and lobsters belong to (11)

7 Complete the table below with the name of the food allergen.

Name of food allergen	Examples of food containing this allergen	Image
	Wheat, rye, oats, barley	
	Crab, lobster	
	Cheese, yoghurt, cream	
	Omelettes, quiche, cakes	
	Salmon, mackerel, haddock, cod	
	Strawberries, kiwi, beetroot, carrot	
	Baked products	
	Scallops, oysters	
	Wholegrain mustard, Dijon mustard, English mustard, salad dressings and sauces	

1.4 Food safety in hospitality and catering

Name of food allergen	Examples of food containing this allergen	Image
	Including walnuts, hazelnuts and cashews	
	Salted peanuts, peanut butter, cakes and biscuits	
	On baked products such as bread, and sushi	
	Soya beans, replacement meat products, dairy replacements	
	Dried fruit, fruit juices, wine	
	Bread, cakes, biscuits	

8 Some bacteria are pathogenic (harmful). Place these pathogenic bacteria in the correct row of the table below to match where they come from (their source).

Bacillus cereus   **Listeria**   **Campylobacter**   **Salmonella**
Clostridium perfringens   **Staphylococcus aureus**   **E. coli**

Name of pathogenic bacteria	Source – where do these bacteria come from?
	Ready meals Untreated dairy products
	Cooked rice and pasta dishes Meat and vegetable dishes
	People – these bacteria can live on the skin Untreated milk
	Raw meat and poultry Milk and milk products
	Raw and undercooked meats Untreated milk
	Eggs (except British Lion mark) Poultry
	Raw meat Soil from root vegetables

Short-answer exam-style practice questions

1 a Name **two** types of harmful (pathogenic) bacteria.

....

.... [2]

Hint

Questions asking you to **name** or **list** require only short answers; full sentences are not needed. Always check to see how many marks are available for each question and how many writing lines have been provided – this is your clue to how much detail is needed.

   b List **two** conditions that bacteria need in order to multiply.

....

.... [2]

2 a The number of people with special dietary needs is increasing.

   If you are catering for someone who is intolerant to gluten, name **two** ingredients they cannot eat.

....

.... [2]

b As well as gluten, other foods may cause intolerances. What is meant by the term 'food intolerance'?

....

....

....

....

....

....[3]

c Name **two** foods/substances other than gluten that people may be intolerant to.

....

....[2]

3 Give any **three** symptoms of food-induced ill health.

a ....

b ....

c ....[3]

4 Name **two** visible and **two** non-visible symptoms of food-induced ill health.

a Visible symptoms:

....

....

b Non-visible symptoms:

....

....[4]

5 Food contamination can be caused in several ways – for example, from physical and chemical sources. Place each of the **four** sources below into the correct column of the table.

waterproof plaster   **cleaning fluid**
insecticide   **hair**

> **Hint**
> Always answer questions like these, even if you are not sure of the answer. A good guess might get you a mark. If you do not attempt the question, the only mark you can achieve is zero!

Physical source	Chemical source

[4]

6 Temperature control is very important to keep food safe.

Label the following temperatures a–d on this thermometer.

a Temperature danger zone
b Fridge temperature
c Freezer temperature
d Safe temperature for reheating food   [4]

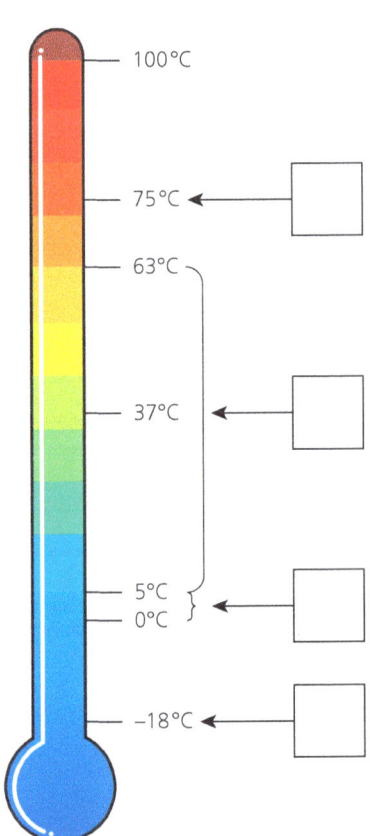

1.4 Food safety in hospitality and catering

7 Ideally food should be served to customers as soon as it is cooked, using clean utensils. Outline **two** reasons why this is important for food safety.

a ....

....

b ....

.... [4]

Hint
Always read the questions carefully. This question is about why hot food should be served hot, and why clean utensils should be used. The best way to answer this question is to use part (a) to outline why hot food should be served as soon as it is cooked and part (b) to outline why clean utensils are important.

Sample answer	Analysis/comment
a If the food is served straight away, bacteria do not have time to grow. If the food is served hot, it will be out of the temperature danger zone, so bacteria are unable to multiply. b Clean utensils can't spread bacteria onto the food. Clean utensils can't spread any allergens onto the food.	This sample answer is very good as it covers both parts of the question; it has two separate points on why the temperature of the food is important and two on why it's important to use clean utensils when serving the food. It is a well-balanced answer that covers both parts of the question and so would gain full marks: 4/4.

8 What is the name of the government worker who can inspect food premises at any reasonable time?

Outline **three** checks this person may make during one of these inspections.

Name of worker:

....

Three checks:

....

....

....

....

....

.... [4]

9 Ideally elbow taps should replace hand-operated taps in the kitchen. Outline **two** reasons why this may help to reduce cross-contamination.

a ....

....

....

b ....

....

....[2]

Long-answer exam-style practice questions

1 Correct food storage is important in order to prevent ill health.

Explain where and at which temperatures food should be stored safely in the kitchen.

Plan your answer

Question context and requirements

- Think about what the question is asking. It has the command word **explain**, so you need to provide details and reasons in your answer. Giving examples in your answer to an explain question will also help you gain more marks.
- When planning your response, first think about the three main areas in the kitchen where food is stored: the fridge, freezer and cupboards (ambient storage). Make sure you learn the ideal temperatures of these three storage areas.
- In terms of structuring your response, take each storage place (fridge, freezer, cupboards) and write a few sentences on how food should be stored safely in each, giving reasons why with examples of foods.

Sample answer – weak response

Food should be stored in the fridge or freezer to stop or slow down the growth of bacteria.

Analysis/comment

This answer is weak and likely to score no more than 2/6 marks. There is a brief explanation of how chilling and freezing foods affects bacteria, but it is too short. It misses out ambient storage and also doesn't mention the actual temperatures in °C. There are no examples of which types of foods should be stored where. Also missing is what is happening to the bacteria/other micro-organisms in the fridge, freezer or cupboards.

1.4 Food safety in hospitality and catering

> **Sample answer – strong response**
>
> Food should be stored in either the fridge, freezer or in a food cupboard.
>
> As soon as the food arrives at the kitchen, it should be stored at the correct temperature.
>
> The fridge temperature is from 0°C to below 5°C. Perishable foods such as fresh meat and cheese should be stored in the fridge to slow down bacterial growth.
>
> The freezer temperature is −18°C or below. Perishable foods such as meat, fish and prepared vegetables may be stored in the freezer to stop bacteria and other micro-organisms from growing.
>
> A food cupboard will be at room temperature, at around 20°C (ambient temperature). Non-perishable foods such as canned foods and dried pasta should be stored here, as bacteria do not grow in these foods.
>
> **Analysis/comment**
>
> Read the strong response and notice how much better it is than the weaker one; it answers all aspects of the question. This response would be awarded full marks: 6/6.
>
> It covers all three places food should be kept in the kitchen – fridge, freezer and food cupboards – and gives the temperatures of all of these places. It also includes the term 'ambient temperature'.
>
> In addition, for all three areas, it gives correct examples of foods that should be kept in each place and explains why.

Now write your own answer.

....

....

....

....

....

....

....

....

....

....

....

....

....

....[6]

2 Describe the main roles and responsibilities of an Environmental Health Officer (EHO).

> **Hint**
> This question has the command word **describe**, which means 'to give an account in words' and 'provide an appropriate amount of information with detail'. It can also mean to provide the 'main features'. As part of your revision, you should have learned the roles and responsibilities of an EHO to be able to answer this question well. To gain full marks, you could choose four roles to describe with good detail and examples, or you could choose five or more responsibilities and describe these in less detail.

[8]

3 Complete the table below with **four** visible and **four** non-visible signs and symptoms of food-induced ill health.

Visible signs and symptoms	Non-visible signs and symptoms

[8]

4 A restaurant was expecting a food order from its usual supplier, but the commis chef would not accept the order as it failed some of her food safety checks.

Food safety check	Pass/Fail	Notes
Food storage	Fail	Both raw and cooked prawns were stored in the same box.
Food temperatures	Pass	
Cleanliness of vehicle	Fail	The van was dirty inside and out.
Expiry dates on foods	Pass	

Review the information in the table and suggest the changes needed to ensure future orders are accepted.

a Change 1:

....

....

....

.... [2]

b Change 2:

....

[2]

c Expiry dates on food can be either 'best before' or 'use by'. Explain the differences between these two expiry dates.

....

[2]

1.4 Food safety in hospitality and catering

5 Cross-contamination is the process by which a substance that is dirty or harmful spreads from one place to another.

Explain the difference between direct contamination and indirect contamination, and how these may be prevented.

> **Hint**
> This question has the command word **explain**, which means to set out the facts and the reasons for them, make them known in detail, and make them plain and clear. As part of your revision, you should have learned about the different types of cross-contamination to be able to answer this question well. To gain full marks you could give a detailed explanation of cross-contamination, and then give two detailed and clear examples of both direct and indirect contamination.

[6]

6 Food labelling regulations tell customers about the food they are buying.

Describe the differences between use-by and best-before dates. Use examples to illustrate your answer.

Hint
This question has the command word **describe**, which means 'to give an account in words' and 'provide an appropriate amount of information with detail'. It can also mean to provide the 'main features'. As part of your revision, you should have learned the differences between use-by and best-before dates. To gain full marks you need to describe, with examples, at least four features of each expiry date and give suitable examples.

....

....

....

....

....

....

....

....

....

....

....

....

....

....

....

....

....

....

.... [6]

Also available...

WJEC Level 1/2 Vocational Award in Hospitality and Catering

Target success with this proven formula for effective, structured revision.

- ✓ Topic-by-topic planner
- ✓ Key content summaries
- ✓ Revision tasks
- ✓ Practice questions
- ✓ Tips and guidance

Our clear and concise approach to revision will help you learn, practise and apply your skills and understanding. Coverage of key content is combined with practical study tips and effective revision strategies to create a guide that can be relied on to build both knowledge and confidence.

Also available as a Boost eBook

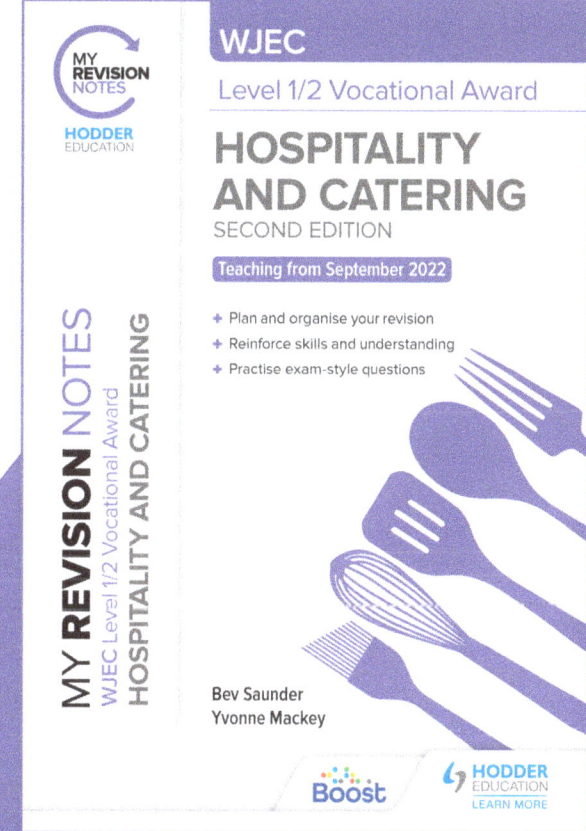

ISBN: 9781398361263

Find out more and order online at www.hoddereducation.co.uk/catering

WJEC Level 1/2 Vocational Award

HOSPITALITY & CATERING EXAM PRACTICE WORKBOOK

Develop the vital skills you need to achieve the best results possible in your exams with this expertly-written Exam Practice Workbook.

Written by experienced teachers and examiners, this write-in Exam Practice Workbook:

- helps you to remember and retrieve information with a range of recall activities for every topic area

- reinforces your understanding and boosts your exam confidence with both short-answer and extended-response exam-style practice questions for you to try and activities that help you to break down the question, plan and review the answer

- allows you to work through on your own either in class or at home, or for last-minute revision.

Includes:
- Recall activities – crosswords, quizzes and more
- Hints and tips on exam technique
- Scaffolded exam-style practice questions
- Example student answers

Also available:
9781398361256 WJEC Level 1/2 Vocational Award in Hospitality and Catering

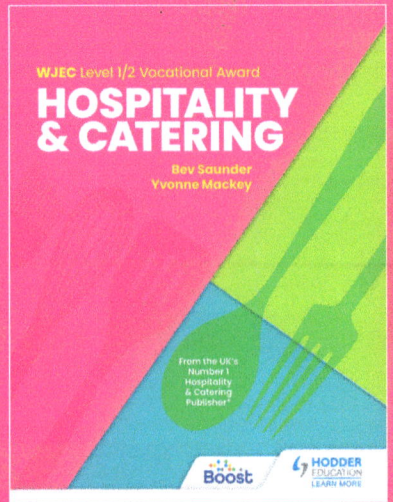

HODDER Education
+44 (0)1235 827827
education@hachette.co.uk
hoddereducation.com

ISBN 978-1-0360-0669-3